CAITLIN CLARK

BASKETBALL DREAMS COME TRUE

Ellen Hicks

ABOUT THE AUTHOR

Ellen Hicks champions children's happiness, health, and education. As a mother of two daughters, she values the role of mentor and nurturing dreams. Ellen's childhood taught her the importance of finding goodness and navigating challenges, inspiring her dedication to helping kids explore interests and develop into kind, curious individuals. A sports enthusiast, Ellen enjoys various sports and the lessons they offer about teamwork and perseverance. She loves sharing stories of inspiring people to guide and motivate others. Now, Ellen pursues her dream of helping children recognize their abilities and grow into happy, confident individuals. Her commitment to children's potential drives her work.

CONTENTS:

INTRODUCTION

BZZZZZT! The buzzer screams, and the crowd goes wild. It's a sea of gold and black—Hawkeye fans on their feet. The score is tied with seconds left on the clock. Caitlin Clark, eyes focused, dodges defenders like she's on a rocket-powered skateboard. She fakes left and bursts right—she's got an open shot! With one second on the clock, Caitlin leaps, basketball held high. It's like the whole world slows down as she shoots. SWISH! The ball flies through the net without even touching the rim.

The crowd explodes! Her teammates rush to the court, hugging her tight. Caitlin beams a smile brighter than any spotlight. This is why she loves basketball—the pure awesomeness of it all. Meet Caitlin Clark, a rising superstar in women's basketball!

Playing sports was a big part of Caitlin's life from the very beginning. It's where she learned so many important lessons, not just about basketball but about life, too.

Caitlin wasn't always a superstar. She grew up in Des Moines, Iowa, where she fell in love with basketball as a kid. She spent hours practicing in her driveway, dreaming of being a legend. Now she's living that dream, dazzling fans in the WNBA.

Her journey wasn't always smooth sailing. She faced setbacks and doubters. But Caitlin never gave up. She practiced harder, ran faster, and came back even stronger. Her secret weapon? A never-give-up attitude and a heart full of grit!

Caitlin is a trailblazer, inspiring girls everywhere to dream big and play hard. Caitlin isn't just a basketball star; she's a super role model for kids everywhere.

Basketball isn't just about winning or scoring points. It's about teamwork, friendship, pushing your limits, and feeling proud of what you can do. It's about confidence and believing in yourself.

This story is for you—the one with big dreams and a heart full of fire. It's about a girl who dared to chase her dreams and who fell down but always got back up. It's about believing in yourself, even when things get tough. Because Caitlin's story isn't just about basketball; it's about chasing your dreams, no matter what they are.

So, how did a girl from Des Moines become one of the biggest names in basketball? Let's rewind the clock and look at Caitlin's early years. We'll meet her family, hear about her first hoops, and discover how her passion for basketball began to grow. Because every superstar has a starting point, and Caitlin's story is proof that with a little bit of love, support, and a whole lot of hard work, amazing things can happen.

CHAPTER 1:
THE EARLY YEARS OF CAITLIN CLARK

Did you know that some of the greatest basketball players of all time, like Michael Jordan and LeBron James, started their careers shooting hoops in their driveways? That was certainly the case for Caitlin Clark. Before she was hitting game-winning shots and breaking records, she was just a kid in Iowa with a big dream and a basketball in her hands. So, lace up your shoes and return to Caitlin's early years in Iowa, where her love for basketball first began.

A STAR IS BORN IN IOWA

In the state of Iowa, located between two rivers, is a city called Des Moines. Des Moines is a friendly city with plenty of places to play. This is where our story begins, in this sports-loving city, on a chilly winter day, January 22, 2002, when a future basketball star named Caitlin Elizabeth Clark was born.

Caitlin grew up in a family that loved sports. Weekends were filled with games of catch and endless hours of shooting hoops. The Clarks were a family that lived and breathed sports! Her dad, Brent, played basketball and baseball in college, and her mom, Anne, came from a family of football coaches. With parents like that, it's no wonder Caitlin and her two older brothers, Blake and Colin, grew up loving sports too. Weekends were filled with backyard games of catch, family trips to cheer on the Iowa Hawkeyes, and afternoons spent perfecting their basketball skills on their home court.

The Clarks weren't just fans but active participants, always encouraging Caitlin and her siblings to try new sports and activities.

Early Signs of Athleticism

Caitlin loved trying new sports, from soccer and softball to swimming, tennis, and even golf! Even as a toddler, Caitlin's parents introduced her to the game with a mini basketball hoop, sparking an early fascination. She loved the thrill of competition, always striving to be the fastest runner, the highest jumper, and the most skilled player. Whether she was dribbling a soccer ball past defenders or smacking a softball over the fence, Caitlin excelled at every sport she tried. But nothing made her heart pound like the sound of her shoes squeaking on the basketball court and the swish of the net as the ball went in. Basketball was her passion and her obsession.

Caitlin loved playing with the boys in her neighborhood, and she more than held her own in pickup basketball games. She wasn't afraid to play tough and often beat the boys! She loved the challenge, the physicality, and the thrill of competition. As Caitlin grew older, her competitive spirit grew stronger. She and her brothers engaged in epic Nerf basketball battles in their basement, getting so heated that her brother once needed staples in his head. She never backed down, always ready for another game.

Caitlin's parents recognized her talent and passion for basketball and nurtured it every step of the way. They drove her to practices and games, cheered her on from the sidelines, and even turned their basement into a makeshift basketball court. They encouraged her to dream big and to never give up on her goals. A home video shows a young Caitlin pretending to be a star athlete, her family cheering her on.

Caitlin's early experiences with sports, especially basketball, instilled in her a love for the game, a strong work ethic, and an unshakeable belief in herself. These qualities would serve her well as she continued her journey toward becoming a basketball superstar.

Early Signs of Competitiveness and Drive

From a young age, Caitlin Clark exhibited a competitive spirit that extended far beyond the basketball court. In the classroom, she was just as determined to excel as she was on the court. Her teachers described her as "very competitive" and "always very, very smart." They recalled her drive and tenacity, evident not just in her athletic pursuits but also in her academic efforts (IndyStar, 2024).

One specific example of Caitlin's competitiveness in academics comes from her participation in a program called Rocket Math in first grade. This program aimed to improve math facts, and Caitlin quickly became highly competitive, striving to be the best in the classroom. Similarly, during a second-grade biography fair project, even though it is unclear who she did the project on, the teacher remembers Caitlin dribbling a basketball while working on it, highlighting her passion for basketball at a young age.

Caitlin's teachers also mentioned a story from her fourth-grade classroom where her facial expressions showed her frustration over something related to math or science. This story further illustrates her competitive spirit and her desire to be the best in everything she does.

Caitlin's early competitiveness and drive were not limited to athletics. She was just as passionate about academics and science and strived to excel in all areas of her life. This well-rounded approach to her education, combined with her natural talent and steady determination, laid the foundation for her future success as a student-athlete.

One of the Boys

Caitlin wasn't always the star you see today. When she was a young girl, there weren't a lot of basketball teams just for girls, so she found herself playing in the boys' leagues. Imagine being one of the few girls on a team of boys! It was a real challenge, and Caitlin had to work twice as hard to prove she belonged.

Playing with the boys made Caitlin tougher and taught her a whole new level of grit. They were bigger and stronger, so she had to be quicker and smarter to keep up. She learned to handle the ball like a pro, see the whole court, and make split-second decisions under pressure. She even had to deal with some people who didn't think a girl could be as good as the boys. Can you imagine how frustrating that would be?

But Caitlin didn't let anything stop her. She kept practicing, kept learning, and kept proving everyone wrong. One time, when she was just five years old, a boy was bullying her during a game, pushing her around because she was smaller. Her grandpa, Bob Nizzi, who was a football coach, was watching from the stands and saw the whole thing. Caitlin's dad, who was her coach, took her out of the game to calm down. But as soon as she was back in, Caitlin didn't go for the ball—she went straight for the bully! She blocked him so hard that he fell out of bounds, and she stood over him to show she wasn't going to be pushed around (Harty, 2023a).

That's when her grandparents knew she was going to be something special. The same passion, toughness, and grit that helped Caitlin stand up to that bully are still a big part of who she is today as one of the best basketball players in the world.

So, next time you're feeling discouraged or facing a tough situation, remember Caitlin's story. Be like her: work hard, believe in yourself, and never stop chasing your dreams, no matter who or what tries to get in your way.

DISCOVERING BASKETBALL—MORE THAN JUST A GAME

Caitlin's love of basketball began in her own yard, under the watchful eyes of her parents. Her dad, Brent, became her first coach and mentor. He taught her the fundamentals of the game: how to dribble, shoot, pass, and defend. But more importantly, he instilled in her a love for the sport and a passion for competition.

For Caitlin, those early days playing basketball were pure magic. She loved the feel of the ball, the sound of the net swishing, and the thrill of running up and down the court with her friends. She played in local leagues, joined her school teams, and spent countless hours practicing in her driveway, often with her brothers as willing—and sometimes unwilling—opponents.

As Caitlin continued to play, her skills blossomed. She developed a lightning-fast crossover dribble, a deadly accurate jump shot, and an incredible ability to see the court and make pinpoint passes. She was a natural scorer, but she also understood the importance of teamwork and making her teammates better.

Of course, there were also challenges along the way. Caitlin faced taller and stronger opponents, experienced tough losses, and had to balance her love for basketball with schoolwork, friendships, and other activities. But she never let these obstacles discourage her. Instead, she used them as motivation to work harder, practice more, and become the best player she could be.

Caitlin's early basketball days were more than just fun; they were the foundation for her future success. They taught her the power of hard work, dedication, and never giving up. They helped her develop the skills and confidence she would need to compete at the highest level. And most importantly, they instilled in her a deep love for the game that would continue to drive her throughout her career.

FAMILY: THE DREAM TEAM BEHIND THE SCENES

Caitlin's family provided steady support throughout her basketball journey. Her parents attended nearly all of her games, cheering her on from the sidelines. They instilled a love for sports in Caitlin and her siblings from a young age, often joining in on the action. Her father fostered her competitive spirit while teaching her the fundamentals of the game. Her mother described Caitlin's playful and spirited personality, which she maintained even in the face of good-natured teasing from her brothers and cousins, who would sometimes playfully soak her with water balloons during snowball fights (Caruso, 2024).

The competitive spirit in the Clark family extended to sibling rivalry as well. Caitlin is incredibly close with her older brother, Blake, who was also a competitive athlete, playing football at Iowa State University. When home, the two would often engage in intense one-on-one basketball games. Her younger brother, Colin, played basketball with her, and their competitive yet supportive relationship further solidified her love for the game. These sibling showdowns weren't just fun and games; they fueled Caitlin's competitive fire and taught her the importance of resilience. Even when she got hurt during a rough play, she bounced back stronger than ever.

Caitlin's family also provided a constant source of love and emotional support. Her father, recognizing the challenges of fame, advised Caitlin to stay away from social media negativity, shielding her from unnecessary distractions. They instilled confidence in her abilities and encouraged her to pursue her dreams no matter what.

Caitlin's family works together as a team to create a supportive and encouraging environment that nurtures her talent and helps her achieve her goals. They attended her games, coached her, provided emotional support, and, most importantly, instilled a deep love for the game in her. Their combined dedication laid a sturdy groundwork for Caitlin, empowering her to excel as a basketball athlete and achieve the peak of success in her sport.

CAITLIN'S COURTSIDE CHALLENGE:

WHAT'S YOUR PASSION?

Just like Caitlin discovered her love for basketball, we all have passions that spark our interest and make us feel truly alive. What's that one thing that excites you, the thing you could do for hours without even realizing it? Is it sports, music, art, writing, building things, or something else entirely?

Now, here's your chance to showcase your passion! Grab a piece of paper, a notebook, or even your favorite digital tool. Express your passion through art, writing, music, or any other creative way that speaks to you. Draw a picture, write a story, compose a song, or even choreograph a dance—the possibilities are endless! Let your creativity flow and show the world what makes you unique.

Remember, your passion is something to be celebrated and shared with others. Don't be afraid to let your light shine and inspire those around you. Who knows, you might even discover new friends and mentors who share your interests and can help you reach new heights!

So, get out there and embrace your passion! The world is your court, and it's time to make your mark.

LITTLE DREAMS, BIG LEAPS

From shooting hoops at home to becoming a college superstar, Caitlin's basketball journey shows the awesome power of dreams, hard work, and believing in yourself. Her early experiences, like sharpening her skills against boys and overcoming challenges that tested her resilience, only fueled her passion for the game and solidified her determination to succeed. As a young girl, Caitlin already envisioned herself as a WNBA star, a dream captured on a childhood home video that foreshadowed the incredible heights she would reach.

As Caitlin grew, so did her love for the game. Each practice, each game, was a step closer to her dreams. Her natural talent blossomed, fueled by many hours of hard work and an unyielding belief in herself. She sharpened her skills, faced challenges head-on, and never let anything dim her passion. This constant pursuit of excellence would soon push her to new heights.

As you continue to follow Caitlin's incredible journey, you'll witness firsthand how her childhood aspirations blossomed into remarkable achievements, setting the stage for an even brighter future on the court. Get ready to experience the next chapter of her story as she takes the high school basketball world by storm and solidifies her status as a rising star.

She was five years old. She could dribble a basketball. She had great anticipation and seeing the floor, which is one of her greatest attributes today. It's just a marvelous thing to remember that she's wired special. Sometimes, there are special athletes that God has created, and God coaches, and Caitlin Clark is one of those. –Bob Nizzi, former Dowling Catholic football coach

CHAPTER 2:
HIGH SCHOOL HEROICS

Caitlin Clark, always with a basketball in hand, even in high school, was known for her infectious smile and the pure joy she brought to the court. Every dribble, every shot, every pass fueled her dreams of being one of basketball's greats. Her love for the game powered her dedication and many hours of practice. Behind her infectious smile, Caitlin was a force to be reckoned with—a rising star and a natural talent.

HOMETOWN HERO: DOMINATING THE COURT

In Caitlin Clark's hometown of West Des Moines stands Dowling Catholic High School, a well-respected place known for its strong academics and athletic excellence. Wearing the uniform of the Dowling Catholic Maroons, Caitlin's exceptional talent and dedication would soon make her a household name in Iowa and beyond. Even as a freshman, Caitlin dazzled on the court, averaging 15.3 points and earning All-State honors (Villa, 2017). As a sophomore, Caitlin's game truly began to blossom, and her stats soared to new heights, showing that Caitlin was a rising star in Iowa high school basketball. Dowling Catholic's team quickly became the one to watch, largely thanks to their star player.

By age 15, Caitlin was already turning heads, even earning a spot on Team USA's U16 national team. However, her journey wasn't without its challenges. Caitlin's natural athleticism, speed, agility, and leaping ability set her apart, but her intense desire to win sometimes led to emotional outbursts and tantrums on the court. Recognizing this, her coaches at Dowling Catholic, especially Kristin Meyer, began working closely with Caitlin to manage her emotions. They made her watch videos of her body language during games to help her understand its impact on her teammates and overall performance.

Coach Meyer started showing her film of her body language, something the Iowa coaches would later continue. Caitlin was often seen throwing her arms in the air in disgust or clapping loudly in frustration. These sessions were pivotal. She learned to recognize and control her emotional reactions, understanding that her behavior could affect her team's morale. This journey of self-awareness and emotional growth was a significant part of her development as a player.

Statistical Superstar

With every game, she got better and better. As a sophomore, she led her team in scoring, rebounds, and assists, averaging 27 points a game and guiding them to a 20-4 record (Naughton, 2018). Caitlin never stopped pushing herself, and her game improved even more the next year. She set new records in Iowa and nationwide by achieving the highest number of points in a single season in Iowa and hitting the national high school record for the most three-pointers made in a single game. She averaged 32.5 points per game, even when facing double and triple teams. These extraordinary numbers placed her among the elite high school players in the country, drawing comparisons to some of the all-time greats.

By her senior year, Caitlin's shooting skills were legendary, hitting shots from all over the court. Her scoring skills were undeniable, leading the state in both her junior and senior years. Unfortunately, her high school career ended abruptly due to the COVID-19 pandemic, leaving everyone wondering what other records she might have broken. However, even with this unexpected season shortening, Caitlin's legacy at Dowling Catholic was firmly established as one of the greatest players to ever grace the Iowa high school basketball courts. Nevertheless, her incredible scoring ability led her to score a staggering 2,547 career points, ranking her 4th all-time among Iowa basketball players (Linder, 2020).

Even rival coaches were in awe, or disbelief, of her abilities. Scott Dejong, the head coach at Ankeny Centennial High, remarked, "Caitlin Clark is truly one of the best players to have ever come out of Iowa. She can do everything on the court. I've seen many great players over my 35-year career, but she affects winning more than anyone I've seen" (Charles, 2023). Her amazing talent earned her the title of Gatorade Iowa Player of the Year, not just once but twice in a row (Caitlin Clark, Iowa Girls Basketball Player of the Year, 2020)!

These numbers only tell part of the story, however. Beyond the raw statistics, Caitlin Clark's dominance was perhaps best illustrated in a series of unforgettable marquee moments that left fans and opponents alike in wonder.

Marquee Moments

Caitlin's high school career was a highlight reel waiting to happen. In one unforgettable game against Mason City, she shattered expectations, making a jaw-dropping 60 points—a performance that echoed through the state and was felt nationally. The local newspaper proclaimed, "When the ball is in Clark's hands, it's must-watch basketball," and this game was the perfect example of that statement (Bain, 2019).

But Caitlin's brilliance wasn't confined to a single game. During her junior season, she etched her name into the Iowa record books by sinking an astounding 13 three-pointers in a single game. This feat showcased her incredible shooting range and accuracy (Goodwin, 2019). That same season, she also shattered the state tournament single-game scoring record with a remarkable 42-point outburst, leaving fans and opponents alike in disbelief of her offensive firepower (Lawhon, 2019).

Her dominance wasn't just about scoring, either. In a game against Southeast Polk, Clark showcased her all-around skills, recording a triple-double with 29 points, 10 rebounds, and 10 assists, proving that she was far more than just a scorer (Morey, 2024). These were just a few of the many marquee moments that defined Caitlin Clark's high school career, leaving an enduring legacy of excellence on the Iowa basketball landscape.

While her basketball achievements received headlines, Caitlin's character and values were equally impressive, making her a true role model for young athletes everywhere.

Beyond the Game

Caitlin wasn't just a basketball star in high school; she excelled in the classroom, maintaining an impressive 3.86 GPA (Caitlin Clark, Iowa Girls Basketball Player of the Year, 2020). She even played a little in varsity soccer during her freshman and sophomore years, scoring an impressive 23 goals a year before focusing solely on basketball.

But beyond academics and athletics, Caitlin was a well-rounded individual and a good example for her peers. She wanted to be a good teammate and someone younger kids could look up to. She cherished the opportunity to inspire others, often taking the time to talk with young fans after games. While the attention felt a bit strange for her, remembering her own childhood admiration for her cousins and their varsity basketball teammates, she embraced the responsibility of being a role model even while still in high school.

Caitlin's character shone through in her actions off the court. She was known for her willingness to help others, even volunteering to clean up the bleachers after games. Caitlin's commitment to her community was evident in her volunteer work at a local food pantry, animal shelter, the Special Olympics, and at a children's hospital in her hometown. Dowling Catholic Principal Matt Meendering recalls, "That was the kind of kid she was and is. It's about leaving something better than when you got there" (Johnson, 2023). Through her actions and words, Caitlin Clark embodied the spirit of a true role model, inspiring others both on and off the court.

Practice Makes Perfect

Caitlin's success didn't come easy. She was known for her strong work ethic and dedication to the game. She spent most of her time in the gym, practicing her shooting, ball-handling, and passing skills. She would often stay after team practices to work on her game, pushing herself to be the best she could be. Coach Meyer observed Caitlin's tireless drive to improve, noting, "She's one who loves a challenge and then responds to it" (Olson, 2024). Her hard work paid off, and her skills grew a lot every season, as seen in her stats.

This relentless pursuit of perfection wasn't without its moments of struggle. Caitlin's coaches often had to remind her to manage her expectations of herself and others. They worked on her mental game just as much as her physical skills, helping her develop the resilience needed to handle the pressures of being a top athlete. This constant striving for growth and her natural talent propelled Caitlin to the top of her game.

As Caitlin's high school career came to a close, it was clear that she was destined for greatness. She left Dowling Catholic with a legacy of excellence, inspiring many young athletes and leaving a mark on Iowa high school basketball history. Her journey from a talented freshman to a two-time Player of the Year is a tribute to her hard work, determination, and passion for the game.

As her high school career drew to a close, Caitlin set her sights on the next challenge: taking her talents to the collegiate level.

SETTING SIGHTS HIGH: CAITLIN'S GOALS

Even as a young girl, Caitlin had big dreams. She wasn't just daydreaming; she set clear goals for herself, on and off the basketball court, and actively worked towards them as early as third grade!

On the court, Caitlin dreamed of becoming a basketball superstar. She wanted to be the best player in the state, leading her team to championships and earning recognition as an All-American. But she wasn't just focused on individual achievements. She wanted to elevate her team, improve her teammates, and create a winning legacy at Dowling Catholic. Her competitive spirit drove her to constantly strive for more, to push herself beyond her limits, and to never settle for anything less than the best.

To keep track of her goals, Caitlin even created a dream board in elementary school, filling it with her biggest aspirations, like earning a basketball scholarship and playing in the WNBA—two dreams she's already achieved! She understood that achieving her goals would require dedication, hard work, and perseverance.

Think of setting goals, like planning a road trip. The goals are your exciting destination—the places you want to go. To get there, you need a roadmap. Caitlin's roadmap was filled with practice sessions, games, and learning from her mistakes. Every step she took brought her closer to her goals, just like every mile on a road trip brings you closer to your destination. By setting goals and working hard to achieve them, Caitlin paved her own path to success, which led her to become one of the best basketball players in the world.

FACING THE BUZZER: OVERCOMING CHALLENGES

Even superstars like Caitlin Clark face challenges on their journey to success. It wasn't always smooth sailing for Caitlin during her high school basketball career. Sometimes, her team faced tough losses, even though they were one of the best in the state. But Caitlin never let a loss get her down for long. She used it as fuel to work even harder, to learn from her mistakes, and to come back stronger the next time.

Balancing school and basketball was like a juggling act. Caitlin had to ensure she did her homework and studied for tests while practicing and playing games. She was super organized, making schedules and sticking to them. She knew that being a good student was just as important as being a good athlete.

Like any athlete, Caitlin sometimes faced minor injuries or setbacks. She had sore muscles and sprained ankles occasionally, like all other student-athletes. But she never let that stop her. She listened to her coaches and trainers, rested when needed, and worked hard to recover quickly. She learned that taking care of her body was essential to playing her best.

Caitlin also had to learn to manage her emotions on the court. Her coaches played a crucial role in this aspect of her development. Through consistent feedback and video analysis of her reactions during games, Caitlin gradually learned to harness her competitive energy more effectively, transforming moments of frustration into opportunities for growth.

Being a star player, especially at the level of Caitlin Clark, comes with a lot of pressure. Everyone expects you to be perfect all the time. Caitlin learned to stay positive, even when things got tough. She focused on her goals, trusted her training, and relied on the support of her coaches, teammates, and family to help her through any challenges.

Remember, everyone, even the greatest athletes, faces obstacles. But what sets them apart is their ability to overcome those challenges and keep moving forward. Caitlin Clark's journey reminds you that with hard work, dedication, and a positive attitude, you can achieve your dreams, no matter what obstacles you face.

CAITLIN'S COURTSIDE CHALLENGE:

WHAT ARE YOUR GOALS?

Just like Caitlin Clark set her sights on becoming a basketball star, you can set amazing goals and make your dreams come true! Let's use a secret weapon—the SMART goal framework—to get you started.

Brainstorming Time!

Grab a pen and paper and jot down three things you're super passionate about. Maybe it's playing a musical instrument, learning to code, or even becoming a master chef. Whatever it is, write it down!

Choosing Your Goal

Pick one of those passions and turn it into a SMART goal. Here's what SMART stands for:

- **Specific:** What exactly do you want to achieve? Instead of saying, "I want to be a better artist," say, "I want to draw a portrait of my pet."
- **Measurable:** How will you know you've reached your goal? Instead of saying, "I want to read more," say, "I want to read 20 books this year."
- **Achievable:** Is your goal realistic? Don't aim for the moon if you're just learning to walk. Start with smaller steps and work your way up.
- **Relevant:** Does your goal matter to you? Make sure it's something you truly care about that will make you excited to get out of bed in the morning.

- **Time-bound:** When do you want to achieve your goal? Give yourself a deadline to stay motivated and focused.

Once you have answered all these questions, your goal is complete, and it's time to make a plan to achieve it!

Action Plan Time!

Now that you have your SMART goal, let's break it down. What are the smaller steps you need to take to reach it? If your goal is to draw a portrait of your pet, maybe your steps are:

1. gather drawing materials
2. find a photo of your pet to use as a reference
3. practice drawing different parts of your pet (eyes, ears, nose, etc.)
4. start sketching the portrait

What's one action you can take today to start working towards your goal? Maybe it's gathering your drawing supplies or finding that perfect photo. Take that first step!

Now, just like Caitlin did in third grade, create a vision board or a drawing of your goal. Put it somewhere you'll see it every day to remind yourself of what you're working towards.

You can achieve amazing things with hard work, dedication, and a clear plan. Now, go out there and make the game plan to your dreams!

THE NEXT LEVEL: COLLEGE BOUND

Caitlin Clark's high school years were a whirlwind of basketball brilliance. From her early days as a talented freshman to her record-breaking senior season, she proved time and time again that she was a force of nature on the court. But her success wasn't just about talent; it was about hard work, dedication, and a never-ending pursuit of her dreams.

Caitlin's story teaches us that even the biggest dreams can come true if you set clear goals, work hard, and never give up. She showed us that challenges are just opportunities to grow stronger and that, with the right mindset and support system, anything is possible.

Caitlin's high school chapter ended, but her basketball journey was far from over. Caitlin always had her sights set on even bigger goals and now she decided to take her talents to the next level. But would her incredible skills translate to the faster, tougher college basketball world? Get ready for the next exciting chapter in Caitlin Clark's incredible story!

always expected her to be successful in college. She is a tremendous basketball player, and we saw that throughout her high school years. So, I'm not all that surprised to see the success that she's had. She's a great leader, a great teammate, and she's really making a positive impact on not just the sports world, but I think [on] the world in general. –Kristin Meyer, Caitlin's High School Coach

CHAPTER 3:
HAWKEYE HUSTLE: COLLEGE YEARS

The summer after her junior year of high school, Caitlin's mailbox overflowed with letters from colleges eager to recruit her. Basketball had been Caitlin's whole world, and now, with one more year to go, she had to make a huge choice: which college to pick. Coaches promised scholarships, trophies, and a shot at the pros. It was thrilling but also overwhelming.

As fall approached, Caitlin knew it was time to make her decision. With a mix of excitement and nerves, she dialed the number that would change her life. This was more than just basketball; it was about choosing a new home.

CHOOSING THE HAWKEYES

Caitlin wasn't just good at basketball; she was a superstar! She was one of the best point guards in the whole country, scoring like crazy and making super-smart plays that made coaches go wild. Big-name schools like Texas, Oregon State, Drake, and even basketball giants like Notre Dame wanted her on their teams. But even with all those fancy offers, Caitlin knew where she belonged. She picked the University of Iowa, the home state team she loved.

> **"** *Out of high school, I could have gone really wherever I wanted to," Caitlin said. "I love the University of Iowa, I love the people, I love my team. Being so close to home, I can always see my family. Honestly, there isn't any place better for me, and I truly believe that.* (Leistikow, 2021). **"**

It wasn't just being close by that swayed her. Caitlin was drawn to Iowa's passionate fans, their black and gold spirit filling Carver-Hawkeye Arena with an energy she craved. She did well in loud atmospheres, feeding off the crowd's enthusiasm like a jolt of electricity. "That's one of the reasons I came to Iowa because the support of the women's basketball team is so good. I just thrive off of crazy crowds," Caitlin explained (Tempera, 2024). Plus, Caitlin wanted to do something different. Caitlin saw the potential in the Hawkeyes, a program hungry for greatness. She wanted to build something special and become a Hawkeye legend.

Making this choice wasn't easy. Caitlin had dreamed of playing for the famous UConn Huskies, but they didn't seem that interested in her. Plus, her parents really wanted her to go to Notre Dame. Caitlin attended a Catholic high school, and her family was Catholic, too. Notre Dame fit with their beliefs, and their women's basketball team was ranked 4th in the whole country! It was tempting, for sure. Yet, deep down, Caitlin knew that her heart belonged to Iowa. She saw the potential in the Hawkeyes, a program hungry for greatness, and a coach, Lisa Bluder, who believed in her.

In the end, Caitlin just knew Iowa was where she belonged. She loved everything about the Hawkeyes, even more than trophies or being number one. So, on November 12, 2019, Caitlin made it official: she would be a Hawkeye. It was a choice that changed everything for her and the team.

HAWKEYE HIGHLIGHTS: CAITLIN'S COURT MAGIC

On October 15, 2023, Kinnick Stadium, the place where the Hawkeye football team usually plays, got a super cool makeover and turned into a giant basketball court. A huge crowd of 55,646 fans came to see Caitlin play her first game as a senior, which was more people than ever at a women's college basketball game! (Gonzalez, 2023). Everyone was super excited to see the basketball hotshot in action.

Caitlin was amazing, scoring 34 points, grabbing 11 rebounds, and making 10 assists—that's called a triple-double! She led the Hawkeyes to a big win over DePaul, 94-72. (Gonzalez, 2023). The game was super fun to watch, but it also did something really important: it raised $250,000 for a local children's hospital (Bohnenkamp, 2023).

This awesome game showed just how popular Caitlin was! Everyone wanted to watch her play, and she was making girls' basketball way more popular. She loved the game so much, and it showed, making everyone else fall in love with it too. Even before the season started, all the tickets to her home games were sold out! This proved just how big of a deal Caitlin was and how exciting the future of women's basketball would be.

Caitlin wasn't just a star player; she was a great teammate and leader too. She was always happy when her friends on the team did well, cheering them on and giving them high-fives. She cared more about the team winning than being the star, which made the Hawkeyes play even better together.

During her time in college, Caitlin kept breaking records! She scored the most points in a single season for a woman in NCAA Division I history—a whopping 1,113 points! (Dotson, 2024) And guess what? She scored the most points ever in college basketball, for boys or girls! She's the greatest of all time!

Throughout her college career, Caitlin's exceptional talent and leadership were recognized with many prestigious awards. She was a two-time consensus National Player of the Year, earning accolades like the Naismith Trophy, the Wooden Award, and the Wade Trophy. Her dominance on the court also earned her three consecutive Big Ten Player of the Year awards and unanimous first-team All-American honors.

CAITLIN'S STATS:

- **CAREER POINTS:** 3,685 (NCAA DIVISION I RECORD)
- **CAREER ASSISTS:** 1,000+
- **CAREER REBOUNDS:** 950+
- **SINGLE-GAME SCORING RECORD:** 49 POINTS
- **SINGLE-SEASON 3-POINTERS MADE:** 201 (NCAA DIVISION I RECORD)
- **SINGLE-SEASON SCORING RECORD:** 1,113 POINTS (NCAA DIVISION I WOMEN'S RECORD)

CAITLIN'S BIGGEST ACHIEVEMENTS:

- **2X CONSENSUS NATIONAL PLAYER OF THE YEAR (2023, 2024)**
- **3X BIG TEN PLAYERS OF THE YEAR (2022, 2023, AND 2024)**
- **2X NAISMITH TROPHY WINNER (2023, 2024)**

Caitlin wasn't just famous in basketball; she was like a superhero! Everyone knew her name, even people who didn't watch basketball. Her awesome moves and super fun style of play style excited everyone, and all the games she played were sold out. She changed how people saw women's basketball, and now it was cool and exciting. She inspired lots of kids to dream big and play their hearts out.

OVERCOMING OBSTACLES

Being a Hawkeye wasn't always easy for Caitlin. Like anyone else, she had tough times. Remember the pandemic? When she was a freshman, it turned her basketball world upside down. Games were canceled, and even when they did play, the stands were empty. For Caitlin, who thrived on the crowd's energy, this was a major challenge. But she didn't let it stop her. She found ways to stay motivated and focused, even without the roar of the fans.

It wasn't just the pandemic that threw obstacles in her path. Injuries, too, tried to slow her down. When she hurt her ankle in her junior year, it was really painful, but Caitlin was tough as nails. She played through the pain, refusing to let it ruin her progress. And then there were those tough losses, especially in the NCAA tournament, they stung. But instead of focusing on the negatives, Caitlin used those setbacks as fuel, analyzing her mistakes and vowing to come back stronger. She learned to be mentally tough, shake off missed shots and bad games, and keep her head high.

As her star rose, so did the expectations and the pressure to be perfect. The whole nation watched her every move, and some people even tried to bring her down with mean comments online. Once, during a rivalry game with Iowa State, the crowd chanted, "Overrated!" But Caitlin didn't let that stop her. Instead, she channeled that negative energy into an incredible performance, scoring 42 points and leading her team to victory (Hall, 2023). It was a reminder that obstacles can make you stronger if you refuse to let them define you.

Caitlin's journey proves the power of perseverance and a positive attitude. She learned that setbacks aren't roadblocks but stepping stones on the path to greatness. She embraced the challenges, used criticism as motivation, and never lost sight of her dreams. Her story reminds us all that we can overcome anything if we have the courage to keep going, the strength to believe in ourselves, and the determination to turn every obstacle into an opportunity for growth.

LEADING THE WAY: CAITLIN'S SUPERSTAR POWER

A Hawkeye Hero

Caitlin wasn't just an exceptional player; she was a star for the Hawkeyes! Her amazing skills and awesome energy made the team super strong. Before Caitlin came, the Hawkeyes were good, but they hadn't gone really far in a long time. With Caitlin on the team, they became one of the best in the whole country and even went to the Final Four twice! Caitlin was so excited to watch that she got everyone interested in the Hawkeyes, even people who didn't usually watch girls' basketball. She was the star of the team, and she inspired lots of other girls to start playing basketball, too.

Basketball Fever

In 2024, everyone talked about Caitlin during March Madness, the biggest college basketball tournament! So many people watched her games on TV that they broke records, and even folks who didn't usually watch basketball became huge fans (McCaskill, 2024). Families gathered around their TVs, cheering for Caitlin and the Hawkeyes, sparking conversations about how awesome and talented women's basketball players are.

The excitement wasn't just limited to college basketball, either. During the WNBA draft, people were so excited to see where Caitlin would end up that they crashed the WNBA website trying to watch! And even the NBA saw a bump in viewership when she appeared on broadcasts. It seemed like everyone wanted a piece of the Caitlin Clark effect!

Back in Iowa City, Caitlin's popularity was like a gold rush! Every home game was sold out, and people were buying Hawkeye gear like crazy. It proved that girls' sports are just as exciting as boys' sports and that they can bring in lots of money and fans. Caitlin was like a shining star, making everyone excited about women's basketball and making it even better for the future.

A True Leader

Caitlin wasn't just a leader on the court; she was a leader off the court, too. She worked harder than anyone else, always trying to get better. She was always the first one to practice and the last one to leave. Her hard work made everyone else on the team want to work hard, too. Even when things got tough, she always stayed positive and cheered everyone on. She made the team feel like they could do anything. Caitlin showed girls and boys everywhere that they can do anything they set their minds to as long as they work hard and never give up!

Making a Difference

Caitlin used her fame to help others, too. In college, she even started the Caitlin Clark Foundation to help young people by ensuring they have access to education, sports, and healthy food. She had a basketball camp for girls where she taught them about the game and inspired them to chase their dreams. She also talks about mental health, telling people it's okay to ask for help if they're feeling sad or worried. Caitlin isn't just a basketball star; she's a real-life hero who uses her power to make the world a better place.

CAITLIN'S COURTSIDE CHALLENGE:

TEAMWORK

Activity: Hawkeye Huddle

Get ready to huddle up like the Hawkeyes! Grab your friends, family, or even your favorite stuffed animals for this team-building challenge.

1. Choose your team name: What's your Hawkeye spirit animal? Are you the Soaring Eagles, the Dazzling Dragons, or the Super Speedy Sloths?

2. Set a goal: Caitlin and her friends work together to win the big game. What's your team's goal? It could be to build the tallest block tower, complete a puzzle the fastest, or even write a cheer for your favorite team.

3. Plan your strategy: Just like the Hawkeyes practice their plays, your team needs a plan. How will you reach your goal? Talk it out and assign roles. Who's the captain, the motivator, or the creative genius?

4. Go for it: It's time to put your teamwork to the test. Remember, the most important part is to have fun and work together, just like Caitlin and her friends.

5. Celebrate your victory: Did you reach your goal? Even if you didn't, celebrate the teamwork and all the fun you had along the way!

Remember: Teamwork makes the dream work! Working together makes even the most impossible tasks easier.

A NEW ERA FOR WOMEN'S BASKETBALL

Caitlin's time in college was a whirlwind of excitement! She broke records, led her team, and inspired thousands of fans. Her incredible talent and never-give-up attitude helped her become one of the best players in the country, and she turned the Hawkeyes into a powerhouse team.

Caitlin's impact was felt far beyond Iowa. She became a superstar, breaking viewership records and turning even those who didn't usually watch basketball into huge fans. The "Caitlin Clark Effect" was so powerful that it even made girls' basketball more popular than ever, proving that girls' sports are just as exciting and important as boys' sports.

But Caitlin's influence went beyond the game itself. She was a leader on and off the court, inspiring others with her hard work and dedication. She even used her fame to help her community and show everyone that even when things get tough, you can overcome any obstacle if you believe in yourself.

Now that she's finished with college, Caitlin is taking her talents to the WNBA. The whole world is watching to see what this amazing athlete will do next!

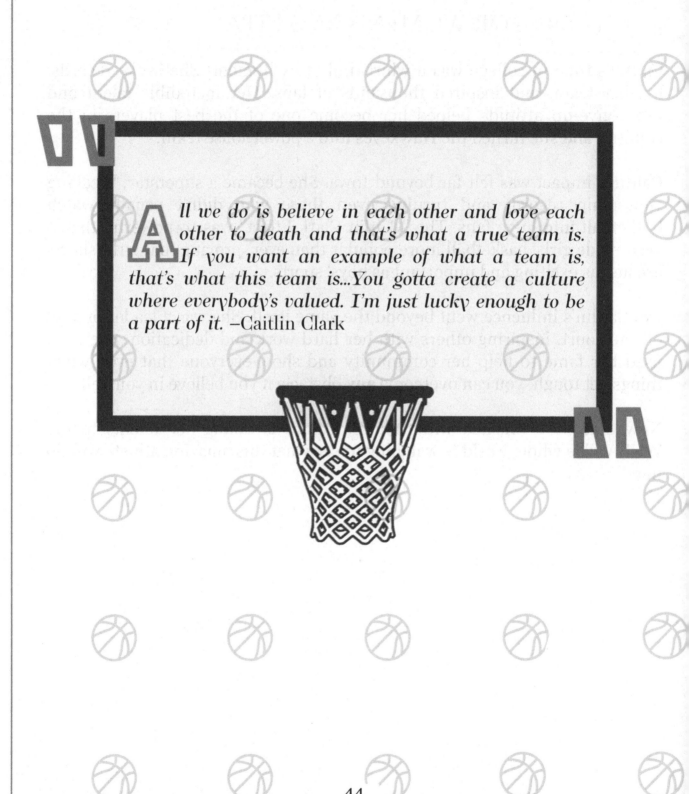

All we do is believe in each other and love each other to death and that's what a true team is. If you want an example of what a team is, that's what this team is...You gotta create a culture where everybody's valued. I'm just lucky enough to be a part of it. –Caitlin Clark

CHAPTER 4:
WNBA DREAMS AND ACHIEVEMENTS

The lights dimmed, a hush fell over the crowd, and Caitlin Clark's heart pounded excitedly. It was draft night, the night every young basketball player dreams of. She had decided to forgo her remaining college eligibility and take the leap into the professional world. Now, all that remained was to wait.

The moment arrived as the commissioner stepped up to the podium. The words echoed through the arena: "With the first overall pick in the 2024 WNBA Draft, the Indiana Fever select...Caitlin Clark!" (ESPN, 2024b). Tears of joy filled Caitlin's eyes as she hugged her loved ones. This was the moment she had been working towards her entire life. Her dream was coming true. The journey to WNBA stardom was about to begin.

The tears flowed freely as Caitlin Clark hugged her family, the number one draft pick's jersey clutched in her hand. It was a moment of pure joy resulting from years of hard work and dedication. But the path ahead was far from clear just a few short months earlier. The decision to leave Iowa and enter the draft was not one taken lightly.

DRAFT DREAMS COME TRUE

On February 29, 2024, Caitlin announced her entry into the WNBA draft, ready to take her game to the next level. Hawkeye fans were sad to see her go but excited for her future. The 2024 draft was highly anticipated, as it marked the first time in years that fans could attend in person. Tickets for the New York City event sold out rapidly, showcasing the immense popularity of both Caitlin and women's basketball.

Draft night was electric. Caitlin, surrounded by family and friends, felt the energy of the roaring crowd gathered in her hometown. The Indiana Fever held the number one pick, a significant factor in her decision to go pro. The announcement of her selection ignited a wave of elation.

In her introductory press conference, Caitlin expressed her enthusiasm for joining the Indiana Fever (Schutte, 2024):

> *I can't think of a better place for myself to start my career. A place that loves basketball, supports women's basketball and an organization that really does things the right way and has a championship pedigree. So, I'm just thankful that they have a belief in me... Couldn't be happier to be here.*

Caitlin was aware of the challenges that awaited her in the WNBA, but she was ready. She was determined to prove that she was more than just a college star—she was a WNBA star in the making. Her adventure was just beginning, and Caitlin was determined to make it unforgettable.

ROOKIE SEASON: TRIAL BY FIRE

Caitlin was now officially an Indiana Fever player! The team was thrilled to have her, and she was eager to contribute to their success. But being a rookie in the WNBA was like starting a new school—everything was different and much tougher. WNBA legend Diana Taurasi acknowledged this transition, stating, "Reality is coming. You look superhuman playing against some 18-year-olds, but you're going to come play with some grown women that have been playing professional basketball for a long time" (Andres, 2024).

The WNBA stands out for its swift transition from college to the professional league for rookies. Following the national championship, the draft occurs approximately a week later, with training camp commencing just two weeks after that. During this period, rookies relocate to a new city, engage in multiple media commitments, and complete remaining college coursework, leaving scarce time for relaxation or even a brief nap (Schnell, 2024). Caitlin faced a very tough schedule, with minimal breaks between games against some of the league's toughest opponents.

Imagine trying to learn all the plays and get to know your new teammates in just a few days while facing an unprecedented gauntlet of a schedule. That's exactly what Caitlin had to do. There wasn't much time to practice before the season officially started that May and the Fever's schedule was packed with games against some of the best teams in the league. It was like a non-stop basketball boot camp. The other teams knew Caitlin was a scoring machine, so they did everything possible to stop her. Sometimes, two or even three players would guard her simultaneously. Plus, the referees made a few calls with people scratching their heads. It was a lot to deal with, but Caitlin didn't back down.

Despite all the challenges, Caitlin showed everyone what she was made of. In her first ten games, she still showed that she was a talented player. She led all the rookies in scoring, assists, and rebounds—that means she was not only scoring points but also helping her teammates score and grabbing rebounds like a champ! Her amazing performance earned her the "Rookie of the Month" award in May (Pickman, 2024b). To be fair, she also led the league in turnovers as her teammates adjusted to her unique style of play.

Even though Caitlin was doing great, the Fever as a team were still trying to figure things out. They were like a puzzle that hadn't quite come together yet.

They needed more time to practice together and build trust on the court. This often meant Caitlin had to adjust her game, which wasn't always easy.

SHINING BRIGHT: CAITLIN'S WNBA IMPACT AMIDST ADVERSITY

As the season progressed, the Fever started to gel as a team, and Caitlin's turnovers decreased. Her numbers on the court remained amazing! She kept scoring many points, getting rebounds, and making awesome passes to help her teammates score, too. She even broke some records! In just 15 games, she achieved a groundbreaking milestone by becoming the quickest player in the league's history to collect 200 points, 75 rebounds, and 75 assists in her career. And the season wasn't even over yet! Fans everywhere loved watching her play, and she even helped bring in new fans who hadn't watched the WNBA before.

Caitlin's standout performance earned her a spot on the All-Star Team, receiving the most votes of any player, including her rival Angel Reese. This marked the first time two rookies were selected for the All-Star Game, a testament to Caitlin's impact on the league.

In a recent game on July 1st against the Phoenix Mercury, Caitlin led her team to victory. Earned the respect of WNBA legend Diana Taurasi, who changed her tune and now praised her performance and predicted a bright future for the young star. Taurasi acknowledged Caitlin's exceptional talent and love for the game, stating,

> *It's amazing what Caitlin's been able to do in her short career so far." Taurasi said, "It's been nothing short of remarkable. The one thing that I really love about her is that she loves the game. You can tell by the way she plays. It's a purity of the game. And it's refreshing to see.* (Lemoncelli, 2024).

In a mind-blowing performance against the New York Liberty, she scored an awesome triple-double. That means she scored 19 points, grabbed 12 rebounds, and made 13 assists—a jaw-dropping feat that had never been done so quickly by any rookie in the entire league history! Not only that, but it was also the very first triple-double ever for the Indiana Fever (De La Fuente, 2024). Talk about a record-breaking night!

Even when things got tough, Caitlin never gave up. Some people thought she was taking too many shots or not passing enough, but she never let the criticism get to her. She stayed true to herself and kept playing her game. Caitlin always strives to improve, and she's not afraid to put in the hard work to reach her goals. Her positive attitude and never-give-up spirit inspired lots of young girls and boys who were watching her.

Caitlin's popularity helped the WNBA become even more popular, too! Games were selling out, and more people were watching on TV. Her team, the Fever, even saw a big jump in ticket sales and new fans. Other players in the league were excited to have her there. Breanna Stewart, one of the WNBA's biggest stars, was impressed by Caitlin's shooting skills, calling her a "knock-down shooter" (Crawford, 2024). Former league MVP Tina Charles said Caitlin and other new players were "injecting new energy into the league" (Achenbach, 2024).

But even with all the excitement, there was one disappointment. Caitlin didn't make the U.S. Olympic team for the 2024 games. Even though she played amazingly, the coaches said she needed more experience. Many fans were upset, but Caitlin took it like a champ, saying,

> *I think it just gives you something to work for. That's a dream. Hopefully, one day I can be there. I think it's just a little more motivation* (McKessy, 2024).

CAITLIN'S COURTSIDE CHALLENGE:

BEING YOUR OWN CHAMPION

Just like Caitlin inspires us, we can all be champions in our own lives! This challenge is all about embracing the qualities that make Caitlin a true role model—kindness, sportsmanship, resilience, and the courage to chase your dreams.

Here's your game plan:
- Show kindness: Do a random act of kindness today. Share a compliment, help someone in need, or just offer a smile. A little kindness can go a long way!
- Be a good sport: Play fair and cheer on others, whether it's in a game or life. Remember, it's not about winning or losing. It's about how you play the game.
- Use your voice: Stand up for what's right, even when it's hard. Your voice matters, and you can make a difference!
- Identify challenges: What makes you feel discouraged or down? Write it down. Recognizing your challenges is the first step to overcoming them.
- Learn and overcome: Brainstorm solutions, ask for help, and don't give up! Remember, even the biggest challenges can be overcome with the right mindset and support.

Remember: Everyone faces setbacks—even Caitlin had a tough rookie season! But it's how you bounce back that makes you a champion. Be kind, play fair, and keep chasing your dreams. You've got this!

A SEASON OF FIRSTS

Caitlin's first year in the WNBA was a whirlwind of exciting firsts—her first draft, first game, first awards, and even her first triple-double! Even though it wasn't always easy, she learned to play with new teammates, faced tough opponents, and dealt with some setbacks. But just like she did when she was a little girl practicing in her backyard, she never gave up. Caitlin's determination and passion for the game shone through, making her a true inspiration to young athletes everywhere.

Missing out on the Olympic team was a bummer, but Caitlin didn't let it get her down. Instead, it fueled her fire to work even harder and come back stronger than ever. This rookie season was just the beginning of an amazing journey for this incredible athlete. Caitlin's story shows us that with hard work, passion, and a never-give-up attitude, we can all achieve our dreams.

But there's more to Caitlin than just basketball! Get ready to discover what makes her tick off the court, from her favorite hobbies to her unique style. Let's explore the many sides of Caitlin Clark: the basketball star, the role model, and the girl who's just getting started.

I hope people remember me for the way I played with a smile on my face and my competitive fire. They can remember the wins but also the fun me and my teammates had together.
—Caitlin Clark

CAITLIN CLARK
Foundation

CHAPTER 5:
LIFE BEYOND BASKETBALL: CAITLIN'S INFLUENCE

> *When I see Caitlin Clark play, it makes me believe that I can do anything," said 10-year-old Emily, a young basketball player from Iowa. "She's not afraid to be herself and always gives it her all. I want to be just like her when I grow up.*

Emily isn't the only one who looks up to Caitlin Clark. The basketball star inspires young athletes everywhere. But what does Caitlin do when she's not on the court? What are her passions, and how does she use fame to help others?

CAITLIN'S OTHER PASSIONS

You might think all Caitlin does is eat, sleep, and breathe basketball—and she does a lot of that—but she has other interests, too. Just like you might like to paint, play video games, or build with Lego, Caitlin has hobbies that she loves doing when she's not on the court.

One of her favorite things is spending time with her family and friends. She loves hanging out with her parents and siblings, especially going to church with them. Caitlin needs to stay connected to her faith and the people she loves, even with her busy schedule. Caitlin's grounded personality is a testament to her family's influence and strong upbringing.

When she's not with family and friends, Caitlin likes to relax and recharge by hitting the golf course. Caitlin enjoys being outdoors and says golf helps her escape from basketball and takes her mind off everything. Even though it's a different kind of competition, we know Caitlin loves to compete at everything, and she says it helps her build mental toughness, which is important for any athlete.

Did you know Caitlin also plays board games? She told the Washington Post that she loves playing a game called Chameleon, where one player is secretly the "Chameleon" and doesn't know the secret word everyone else is hinting at (Golliver, 2023). For example, if the secret word is "apple," everyone else might say clues like "red," "fruit," or "pie." The Chameleon has to blend in and guess a word that seems to fit without giving themselves away, maybe saying "sweet" or "healthy." It's a fun way for her to relax and use her brain in a different way than on the basketball court.

Another favorite treat of Caitlin's is chocolate chip cookies, which she enjoys whenever possible. Her preference for this classic treat shows her simple, relatable side that fans find endearing.

These hobbies are important to Caitlin because they help her stay balanced and happy. Even though she loves basketball, she needs to have other interests that she can enjoy. It's like having different flavors of ice cream— you don't want to eat just one all the time!

Having different hobbies also helps Caitlin be more creative and well-rounded. It allows her to use different parts of her brain and learn new skills. Plus, it's just plain fun to try new things! So, just like Caitlin, don't be afraid to explore different hobbies and activities. You might discover hidden talents or find something you love more than basketball!

ROLE MODEL ON AND OFF THE COURT

Caitlin Clark is more than just a basketball player; she's a role model who inspires millions of people worldwide. Her tireless dedication and passion for the game are evident in her relentless pursuit of improvement. She arrives at the gym before sunrise, stays late into the night, and constantly challenges herself to reach new heights.

Caitlin's impact, however, goes beyond her work ethic. She's a beacon of positivity, spreading infectious energy that uplifts her teammates and captivates fans. Her genuine smile, celebratory dances, and playful interactions with the crowd create an atmosphere of joy and excitement. Even when faced with setbacks, she maintains a positive attitude, demonstrating resilience and determination that inspires young athletes to persevere through their own challenges. Fans appreciate that she is not afraid to be herself and show her emotions and how she celebrates her accomplishments with her team. After games, win or lose, you can always find Caitlin signing autographs, posing for photos, and chatting with young fans, further solidifying her connection with the community.

For many young girls and women, Caitlin is a trailblazer redefining what's possible in a sport traditionally dominated by men. When she shatters scoring records and leads her team to victory, she shows that girls can compete at the highest level and achieve their dreams. She is a role model who inspires young athletes to believe in their potential regardless of gender.

Caitlin's impact extends beyond the basketball court, as she actively engages with her community and inspires the next generation of athletes. She understands the responsibility that comes with her platform and strives to use it for good. Her goal is to grow the game and show younger girls and boys they can do whatever they want. Her genuine and relatable nature makes her an approachable role model, proving that even superstars can be down-to-earth and kind. She represents the idea that success isn't just about winning games but about positively impacting others and leaving a lasting legacy.

GIVING BACK: CAITLIN'S COMMUNITY IMPACT

Caitlin's big heart doesn't just stay on the basketball court—it extends far beyond the hardwood. Soon after her sudden rise to national stardom, Caitlin established the Caitlin Clark Foundation, a testament to her commitment to uplifting young people and her community. The foundation focuses on three important ideas that Caitlin knows firsthand are essential for success: providing access to sports, ensuring kids have the tools they need to thrive academically, and promoting healthy nutrition so kids can be their best on and off the court.

The Caitlin Clark Foundation's impact is far-reaching. It partners with organizations like Hy-Vee, Scheels, and the University of Iowa to bring its programs to life. The foundation hosts basketball camps where kids can learn new skills, build confidence, and make lasting friendships. Recognizing that a healthy body fuels a sharp mind, the foundation also works tirelessly to combat food insecurity, ensuring all children have the nutrition they need to excel in school and sports. This includes initiatives like partnering with local food banks and providing resources for families to access healthy meals.

Caitlin's community involvement extends beyond her foundation. She's a frequent visitor to schools, inspiring students with her story of perseverance and dedication. Her influence goes even further: teaming up with the Coralville Community Food Pantry, she headed a fundraising effort that brought in over $100,000 in donations, making a real difference in the fight against hunger in her hometown (Jane, 2024).

Caitlin's actions speak volumes. She believes that everyone, regardless of age or ability, has the power to create positive change. Just as she uses her basketball talents to lead her team to victory, she uses her platform to uplift her community. By demonstrating compassion and generosity, Caitlin hopes to spark a ripple effect of kindness, inspiring others to follow her lead.

CAITLIN'S COURTSIDE CHALLENGE:

BE A COMMUNITY ALL-STAR

Want to be a community all-star like Caitlin? Here are some ways you can make a difference:

- **Spread the word:** Tell your friends and family about the Caitlin Clark Foundation and its work. You can even share their website or social media pages.
- **Volunteer your time:** Look for opportunities to volunteer at local organizations that support kids' education, sports programs, or food pantries. Every little bit helps!
- **Start a food drive:** Organize a food drive at your school or in your neighborhood to collect healthy snacks and meals for kids in need.
- **Be a mentor:** Offer to tutor a younger student, coach a youth sports team, or simply listen to someone who needs it.
- **Spread kindness:** Remember to always be kind and supportive to those around you. Small acts of kindness can have a big impact!

Remember, even small actions can make a big difference in your community. By working together, we can all be champions for a better future!

A FORCE FOR GOOD ON THE COURT AND BEYOND

Caitlin Clark is more than just a basketball wizard—she's a role model who shows us that we can be successful, kind, and have fun while making a difference in the world. Whether she's sinking a three-pointer, playing a round of golf, or helping kids in her community, Caitlin inspires us all to chase our dreams and be the best versions of ourselves.

Beyond philanthropy, Caitlin Clark's influence extends to the fashion world. A budding fashion icon, Clark's unique style makes waves both on and off the court. From her wardrobe choices to brand collaborations, Clark is redefining athletic fashion.

I don't want my legacy to be, oh, Caitlin won X amount of games or Caitlin scored X amount of points. I hope it's what I was able to do for the game of women's basketball. I hope it is the young boys and young girls that are inspired to play this sport or dream to do whatever they want to do in their lives.
–Caitlin Clark

CHAPTER 6:
CAITLIN'S COLORFUL KICKS: EMBRACING PERSONAL EXPRESSION

Neon green, hot pink, and even a touch of Tiffany blue! Caitlin Clark's shoes, or "kicks," as the old-school "sneakerheads" might say, aren't just footwear—they're a rainbow of colors, patterns, and pure awesome. When she steps onto the court, her footwear steals the show, which amazes everyone. But her shoe game isn't just about looking cool; it's about feeling confident, expressing her unique style, and inspiring others to do the same. She's even designing her own basketball with Wilson, making her the first athlete since Michael Jordan to have that honor!

Caitlin's love for shoes is legendary. From rocking Kobe Bryant's iconic designs to sporting high-fashion collaborations, she's become a trendsetter both on and off the court. She's even landed a huge deal with Nike to create her own signature shoe! Get ready to dive into Caitlin's colorful world of footwear, explore her favorite brands, and discover how her passion for fashion helps her shine even brighter! Lace-up your imagination and step into Caitlin's stylish world!

MORE THAN JUST SHOES: CAITLIN'S SIGNATURE STYLE AND BRAND PARTNERSHIPS

For Caitlin Clark, shoes are more than footwear—they're a canvas for self-expression, a burst of personality that adds a touch of magic to her game. Her shoe collection is a vibrant mix of colors, patterns, and designs, gravitating toward bold, eye-catching choices that mirror her confident and fun-loving personality. One day, she might rock a pair of neon green Kobe 6 Protros, a nod to her basketball idol, and the next, she might step out in the luxurious Tiffany Blue Nike Air Force 1s. Her choices aren't just about how they look; they're about feeling empowered and expressing her individuality on the court.

This unique style hasn't gone unnoticed. Fans and shoe enthusiasts have even created websites dedicated to tracking her in-game footwear and corresponding stats, showcasing the cultural impact of her choices. In fact, her eye-catching style caught the attention of top brands even before she stepped onto the professional court. Prada and Louis Vuitton, two of the biggest names in fashion, reached out to style Caitlin for the WNBA draft and her introductory press conference, respectively. This is a big deal because, typically, only pro athletes who have played for at least five years get noticed by these big brands. But Caitlin's bold and expressive fashion choices stood out from the start.

In a groundbreaking move, Nike signed Caitlin to a multi-million-dollar deal to create her own signature shoe line. This is a major milestone, not just for Caitlin but for women's basketball, signaling the growing recognition and respect for female athletes and their influence beyond the game. Caitlin's signature shoe will reflect her personality and values, incorporating her favorite colors, patterns, and even personal touches that tell her story.

Nike isn't the only brand competing for Caitlin's attention. She's become a sought-after ambassador for diverse companies, from sports giants like

Gatorade and Wilson to car manufacturers like Buick and tech companies like Bose. Caitlin carefully chooses her partners, ensuring they match her interests and values. For example, her love for music made partnering with Bose, a company known for its high-quality headphones, a natural fit.

These partnerships aren't just about looking cool in commercials; they're also a way for Caitlin to earn money and build her brand. With her background as a marketing major in college, she understands the business side of endorsements and uses that knowledge to strategically grow her brand. However, for her, it's not just about the money; it's about using her platform to inspire others and connect with fans who share her passion for sports, fashion, and self-expression.

CONFIDENCE ON YOUR FEET: THE POWER OF PERSONAL STYLE

Have you ever worn your favorite outfit and felt like you could conquer the world? That's the power of personal style! What you wear isn't just about looking good; it's about feeling good. It's a way to show the world who you are, what you love, and what makes you unique.

Caitlin knows this feeling well. Her bold and colorful shoe choices aren't just a fashion statement; they're a way to express her confidence and creativity. When she steps onto the court, she feels unstoppable, ready to take on any challenge.

Your style doesn't have to be the same as Caitlin's to be powerful. It doesn't matter if you love bright colors, patterns, or prefer a more classic look, as long as it makes you feel good and represents who you are.

So, what's your signature style? Do you have a favorite pair of shoes that make you feel like you can fly? Remember, your style is all about you. It's a way to express yourself, boost your confidence, and show the world what you're made of. So rock that outfit, wear those shoes, and be proud of yourself.

CAITLIN'S COURTSIDE CHALLENGE:

DESIGN YOUR DREAM SHOES!

Get ready to unleash your inner shoe designer! Just like Caitlin is creating her own signature shoes, it's your turn to imagine the coolest, most awesome pair of shoes you can dream up. Let's call them your "power shoes" that make you feel unstoppable and ready to take on any challenge.

Here are some questions to get you started:

- **Colors:** What colors make you feel happy and powerful? Are you drawn to bright neons, cool blues, or a mix of everything?
- **Patterns:** Would you want your shoes to have a fun pattern, like stripes, polka dots, or even your favorite animal print? Or do you prefer a solid color that really pops?
- **Materials:** What would your shoes be made of? Soft leather, shiny metallics, or maybe a comfy knit fabric?
- **Special Features:** Would your shoes light up? Have wings? Maybe they'd have your initials or a symbol representing something you love. Get creative!

Now, grab some paper, pencils, crayons, or markers and start sketching! Let your imagination run wild, and don't be afraid to try new things. Imagine yourself wearing your dream shoes on the court, scoring the winning basket, or maybe just walking down the street feeling like a champion. Your shoes reflect you, so make them as unique and awesome as you are!

BE BOLD, BE BRIGHT: EMBRACING YOUR INDIVIDUALITY

Caitlin's passion for self-expression shines through in her vibrant shoe choices, whether she's sporting a classic Nike Kobe design or a bold Tiffany & Co. collaboration. Her shoes are more than just footwear; they reflect her personality, her confidence, and her journey from a small-town girl with big dreams to a WNBA superstar. The world has taken notice of Caitlin's unique style, as evidenced by her historic shoe deal with Nike and numerous partnerships with other top brands. But beyond fashion and fame, it's important to embrace your individuality, express yourself, and not be afraid to stand out. Be confident in your own skin and chase your dreams with passion and flair, just like Caitlin Clark.

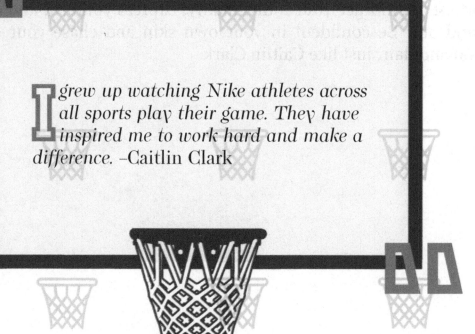

I grew up watching Nike athletes across all sports play their game. They have inspired me to work hard and make a difference. –Caitlin Clark

TIMELINE OF CAITLIN

2007:

At 5 years, begins playing basketball with the boys.

2016:

Scores 23 goals playing soccer as a Freshman in High School.

2013:

In 6th grade, noticed by a recruiter from University of Iowa.

2002:

Caitlin is born in Des Moines, Iowa.

CLARK'S STAR MOMENTS

2023:

Wins her first of two Naismith National Player of the Year Awards. Named the Wooden Award National Player of the Year.

2017:

At 15, plays for Team USA U16 National Team and wins gold.

2024:

2020:

As a high school senior, wins the McDonald's All-American award and is Iowa Miss Basketball. Begins her college career at the University of Iowa.

Set NCAA's career and single-season scoring records. Drafted by the WNBA Indiana Fever. Named to the WNBA All-Star Team.

2019:

Named the Gatorade State Player of the Year.

CONCLUSION

Caitlin Clark's journey from a young girl shooting hoops in her yard to a WNBA superstar proves the extraordinary power of perseverance and strong belief in oneself. It's a story that connects with us, reminding us that even the biggest dreams can be achieved through hard work, dedication, and a neverending pursuit of excellence.

From her early days playing against boys in Iowa to facing the pressures of national stardom, Caitlin's path was far from easy. She encountered obstacles and setbacks, moments of self-doubt and criticism, but she never allowed those challenges to define her. Instead, she used them as fuel to push herself forward, embracing the adversity and emerging stronger, more determined, and more focused than ever before.

Caitlin's story teaches us that setbacks are not roadblocks but stepping stones on the path to greatness. In those moments of struggle, we discover our true strength, resilience, and passionate spirit. Like Caitlin, we can transform adversity into opportunity, using it as a springboard to reach new heights and achieve our wildest dreams.

So, the next time you face a challenge or encounter a setback, remember Caitlin's story. Remember her unstoppable work ethic, unshakable belief in herself, and ability to rise above adversity. Embrace the struggle, learn from your mistakes, and never stop believing in your potential. Because, just like

Caitlin, you have the power within you to achieve anything you set your mind to. The world is waiting for you to shine, so go out there and make your mark!

GLOSSARY

Ambassador: A person who represents a particular brand or organization in a positive way.

Arena: A large enclosed area used for sporting events or entertainment.

Assist: When a player passes the ball to a teammate who then scores.

Athleticism: The natural ability to be good at sports.

Boot camp: A training program that is very intense and difficult.

Competitive edge: The ability to perform better than others, especially in sports or business.

Draft: An event where professional sports teams select new players to join their team.

Dribble: To bounce a ball repeatedly with one hand while running or walking.

Endorsements: A public statement of approval or support, often from a celebrity or well-known person, for a product or service.

Foundation: An organization that uses money to help people or support a cause.

Freshman: A first-year student in high school or college.

GPA (Grade Point Average): A number that shows a student's average grade in school.

Grit: Courage and determination despite difficulty.

Marquee: A large sign over the entrance to a theater or arena. In sports, a "marquee moment" is an important or memorable event.

Perseverance: Continued effort to do or achieve something despite difficulties, failure, or opposition.

Platform: A position of influence or authority that allows someone to share their ideas or opinions with a large audience.

Point guard: A position in basketball; the player is responsible for leading the team's offense and setting up plays.

Rebound: When a player grabs the ball after a missed shot.

Resilient: Able to recover quickly from difficulties or setbacks.

Rookie: A first-year player in a professional sport.

Scholarship: Money given to students to help pay for their education, often because of their academic or athletic skills.

Sophomore: A second-year student in high school or college.

Stats (Statistics): Numbers that measure a player's performance in sports.

Three-pointer: A shot made from beyond a designated line on the basketball court, worth three points.

Trailblazer: A person who is the first to do something and shows others that it is possible.

Trendsetter: A person who starts a new fashion or trend.

Triple-double: A rare achievement in basketball when a player scores double digits in three statistical categories (points, rebounds, and assists) in a single game.

Varsity: The main team representing a high school or college in sports.

WNBA (Women's National Basketball Association): A professional basketball league for women in the United States.

77

REFERENCES

Achenbach, E. (2024, May 20). *Former WNBA MVP sounds off on Caitlin Clark, new players' impact.* Clutch Points. https://clutchpoints.com/wnba-news-former-mvp-sounds-off-caitlin-clark-new-players-impact

Actualizado. (2024, April 18). *Caitlin Clark's coach shares the inspiring story behind her WNBA draft triumph.* MARCA. https://www.marca.com/en/basketball/wnba/indiana-fever/2024/04/18/66213dd1268e950c8b45e4.html

Andres, P. (2024, April 6). *Diana Taurasi dad blunt message for Caitlin Clark on her upcoming WNBA career.* SI. https://www.si.com/college/2024/04/06/diana-taurasi-blunt-message-caitlin-clark-wnba-career

Awards & accolades. (n.d.). Caitlin Clark 22. https://caitlinclark22.com/awards-and-accolades

Bain, M. (2019a, August 5). *"We're almost there": Blue-chip Iowa PG Caitlin Clark is down to three finalists.* The Des Moines Register. https://www.desmoinesregister.com/story/sports/high-school/recruiting/2019/08/05/iowa-point-guard-caitlin-clark-recruiting-three-finalists-iowa-iowa-state-notre-dame/1907572001/

Bain, M. (2019b, November 12). *Analysis: Caitlin Clark has a chance to be the face of Iowa women's basketball.* Hawk Central. https://www.hawkcentral.com/story/sports/college/iowa/bbwomen-recruiting/2019/11/12/analysis-caitlin-clark-has-chance-face-iowa-womens-basketball-lisa-bluder/2577004001/

Bain, M. (2020a, January 24). *Dowling Catholic star Caitlin Clark has lofty goals for her career at Iowa.* The Des Moines Register. https://www.desmoinesregister.com/story/sports/high-school/2020/01/24/shes-not-afraid-cut-nets-down-caitlin-clark-has-lofty-goals-her-career-iowa-hawkeyes-lisa-bluder/4556693002/

Bain, M. (2020b, June 19). *Dowling Catholic's Caitlin Clark named 2020 All-Iowa Girls' Athlete of the Year.* The Des Moines Register. https://www.desmoinesregister.com/story/sports/high-school/2020/06/18/dowling-catholics-caitlin-clark-named-2019-20-all-iowa-girls-athlete-year/3207349001/

Bennet, E. (2024, February). *MSN.* MSN Sports. https://www.msn.com/en-us/sports/other/caitlin-clark-s-ascent-from-childhood-prodigy-to-women-s-basketball-stardom/ar-BB1hSnYH?token=970ec4b7067e4d95a89fac2854daf3d4

Bohnenkamp, J. (2023, October 16). *Clark's triple-double highlights game at Kinnick. Women's basketball record crowd of 55,646 shows up.* Iowa Public Radio. https://www.iowapublicradio.org/ipr-news/2023-10-16/caitlin-clark-triple-double-kinnick-iowa-womens-basketball-record-crowd

Borelli, S. (2024, February 6). *Three reasons Caitlin Clark is so relatable - whether you're a fan, player or parent.* USA Today. https://www.usatoday.com/story/sports/ncaaw/2024/02/06/caitlin-clark-iowa-relatable-young-fans/72486694007/

Briskin, L. (2024, March 29). *10 things you didn't know about Caitlin Clark, basketball's newest superstar.* SELF. https://www.self.com/story/caitlin-clark-facts

Caitlin Clark. (n.d.). Britannica Kids. https://kids.britannica.com/students/article/Caitlin-Clark/641778?token=970ec4b7067e4d95a89fac2854daf3d4

Caitlin Clark - Iowa girls basketball player of the year. (2020). Gatorade. https://playeroftheyear.gatorade.com/winner/caitlin-clark/37695

Caitlin Clark reveals which sport she would play if basketball did not exist for her. (2024, April 25). MARCA. https://www.marca.com/en/basketball/wnba/indiana-fever/2024/04/26/662ace0546163fa0948b457f.html

Caitlin Clark Shoes. (n.d.). Flight Club. https://www.flightclub.com/collections/caitlin-clark

Caitlin Clark's bold shoe selection stole the spotlight in her WNBA debut. (2024, May 14). MARCA. https://www.marca.com/en/basketball/wnba/indiana-fever/2024/05/15/6643fd7c268e3ef5418b45c5.html

Caitlin Clark's faith family proud. (2023, April 3). Diocese of Des Moines. https://www.dmdiocese.org/news/caitlin-clarks-faith-family-proud

Caitlin Clark's reported $28 million Nike deal is richest sponsorship contract for a women's basketball player. (2024, April 24). KCCI. https://www.kcci.com/article/caitlin-clark-nike-shoe-deal/60584556

Caruso, S. (2024, April 9). *All about Caitlin Clark's parents, Brent and Anne Nizzi-Clark.* People. https://people.com/all-about-caitlin-clark-parents-8597994

Cavanaugh, S. (2024, April 16). *"She set that goal as a second-grader" - Caitlin Clark's high school coach shoutout to No.1 pick for nailing her WNBA dream.* Sportskeeda. https://www.sportskeeda.com/us/wnba/news-she-set-goal-second-grader-caitlin-clark-s-high-school-coach-shoutout-no-1-pick-nailing-wnba-dream

Charles, D. (2023, May 10). *Caitlin Clark's 8th grade basketball highlight videos resurface.* BroBible. https://brobible.com/sports/article/caitlin-clark-8th-grade-highlight-videos/

Choi, J. (2024, April 22). *Caitlin Clark's off-the-court style is totally stunning.* Glam. https://www.glam.com/1566346/caitlin-clark-stunning-off-the-court-style/

Clark named Naismith Player of the Year. (2024, April 3). University of Iowa Athletics. https://hawkeyesports.com/news/2024/04/03/clark-named-naismith-player-of-the-year/

Crawford, B. (2024, May 20). *Caitlin Clark earns Breanna Stewart's praise after New York Liberty top Indiana fever.* 247Sports. https://247sports.com/article/caitlin-clark-earns-breanna-stewarts-praise-after-new-york-liberty-top-indiana-fever-231981143/#:~:text=Clark%20scored%2022%20points%20on

Darvin, L. (2024, May 9). *The WNBA was not ready for the "Caitlin Clark effect."* Forbes. https://www.forbes.com/sites/lindseyedarvin/2024/05/04/the-wnba-was-not-ready-for-the-caitlin-clark-effect/

Davidson, K. A. (2024, May 18). *Caitlin Clark is not overhyped—but the WNBA was underestimated.* MSNBC. https://www.msnbc.com/opinion/msnbc-opinion/liberty-game-today-wnba-caitlin-clark-breonna-stewart-rcna152838

De La Fuente, H. (2024, July 6). *Caitlin Clark becomes first rookie in WNBA history to record triple-double.* CNN Sports.

https://www.cnn.com/2024/07/06/sport/caitlin-clark-wnba-triple-double-record-spt-intl/index.html

Dixon, E. (2024, May 22). *Caitlin Clark gets signature basketball line as part of Wilson endorsement deal.* Sports pro Media. https://www.sportspromedia.com/news/caitlin-clark-wilson-endorsement-deal-wnba-michael-jordan/

Dochterman, S. (2024, January 27). *Iowa's Clark nearing big ten scoring record.* The New York Times. https://www.nytimes.com/athletic/5231998/2024/01/27/caitlin-clark-big-ten-scoring-record-iowa-nebaska/

Donald, R. (2024, February 10). *The high school years: Caitlin Clark before the Iowa Hawkeyes.* Hawkeyes Wire. https://hawkeyeswire.usatoday.com/gallery/iowa-hawkeyes-womens-basketball-caitlin-clark-the-high-school-years/

Dotson, K. (2024, March 26). *Caitlin Clark sets women's record for points in a single season as Iowa punches ticket into sweet 16.* CNN. https://www.cnn.com/2024/03/25/sport/iowa-womens-basketball-ncaa-tournament-spt/index.html

Drenon, B. (2024, May 21). *Caitlin Clark lands historic endorsement deal with Wilson.* BBC. https://www.bbc.com/news/articles/c988vqpjp7qo

Dye, N. (2024, May 8). *Caitlin Clark shares sweet home video of her pretending to be a star athlete as a kid.* People. https://people.com/caitlin-clark-shares-home-video-pretending-star-athlete-as-a-kid-exclusive-8644242

Eickholt, D. (2020, May 2). *'Get back to the playoffs: Caitlin Clark's sets goals for rookie season during Indiana fever media day.* Hawkeye Insider. https://247sports.com/college/iowa/article/get-back-to-the-playoffs-caitlin-clarks-sets-goals-for-rookie-season-during-indiana-fever-media-day-231311346/

ESPN. (2024a, March 22). *Caitlin Clark tells her whole hoops story – from childhood to Iowa to the WNBA draft.* YouTube. https://youtu.be/NoOZgZpKtog?si=lMTaqA2PzkaUHR1f

ESPN. (2024b, April 15). *Caitlin Clark selected no. 1 overall by the Indiana Fever.* YouTube. https://youtu.be/ew-uK9AeEP0?si=EXGW74shADiU1qHC

Famous Philanthropists: Caitlin Clark. (2024, April 15). Project Heart. https://myprojectheart.org/blog/famous-philanthropists-caitlin-clark

Feinberg, D. (2024, April 15). *Caitlin Clark's young dream of playing in the WNBA is set to become reality.* NBC Chicago. https://www.nbcchicago.com/news/sports/caitlin-clark-wnba-dream-indiana-fever/3410883/

Fenton, F. P. (2024, April 17). *Caitlin Clark "tries to maximize her God-given talents," coach says.* Catholic News Agency. https://www.catholicnewsagency.com/news/257414/caitlin-clarks-former-coach-says-she-tries-to-maximize-her-god-given-talents-and-share-those-with-the-world

Flores, E. (2024, April 19). *Caitlin Clark's exploding value: List of fever star's endorsements and contract details.* USA Today. https://www.usatoday.com/story/sports/wnba/2024/04/19/caitlin-clark-contract-details-endorsement-lists/73375721007/

Forde, M. (2023, April 1). *Caitlin Clark's dad shares viral story about Iowa star playing basketball against boys.* Athlon Sports. https://athlonsports.com/college-basketball/caitlin-clark-iowa-dad-boys-aau-final-four#:~:text=According%20to%20Front%20Office%20Sports

Frommer, F. (2024, June 9). *Caitlin Clark - Biography, stats, height, record, & facts.* Britannica. https://www.britannica.com/biography/Caitlin-Clark

Gallo, C. (2024, February 28). *The mental hack that makes Caitlin Clark a basketball superstar.* https://www.inc.com/carmine-gallo/the-mental-hack-that-makes-caitlin-clark-a-basketball-superstar.html

Garcia, R. (2024, February 15). *Dowling girls basketball reflects on Caitlin Clark's legacy: "She's a great role model."* Weareiowa.com. https://www.weareiowa.com/article/sports/ncaa/iowa-hawkeyes/dowling-catholic-girls-basketball-caitlin-clark-kristin-meyer-coach/524-d2beb05e-2274-48dc-b727-80bb1a2d58c4

Gibson, K. (2024, April 9). *All about Caitlin Clark's 2 siblings, Blake and Colin Clark.* People. https://people.com/all-about-caitlin-clark-siblings-8620008

Goldkamp, T. (2024, June 23). *Caitlin Clark sets new WNBA career high vs. Chicago Sky.* On 3. https://www.on3.com/her/news/caitlin-clark-sets-new-wnba-career-high-for-assists/

Goldsberry, J. (2024, May 4). *Caitlin Clark plays first WNBA game to sold-out arena.* Washington Examiner. https://www.washingtonexaminer.com/sports/2991523/caitlin-clark-plays-first-wnba-game-to-sold-out-arena/?utm_source=google&utm_medium=cpc&utm_campaign=Pmax_USA_Magazine_21-June-Intent-Audience-Signals&gad_source=1&gclid=Cj0KCQjwsuSzBhCLARIsAIcdLm5r8KBdSiptw-bfBlZso4ONKvHZ4oHQht3va3CSyxhGQcRF61CPJ5caAvx5EALw_wcB

Golliver, B. (2023, April 4). What comes next for Caitlin Clark is the hardest part. *Washington Post.* https://www.washingtonpost.com/sports/2023/04/04/caitlin-clark-next-season/

Gonzalez, I. (2023, October 15). *Caitlin Clark, Iowa break women's college basketball attendance record with exhibition game at Kinnick stadium.* CBS Sports. https://www.cbssports.com/womens-college-basketball/news/caitlin-clark-iowa-break-womens-college-basketball-attendance-record-with-exhibition-game-at-kinnick-stadium/

Goodwin, C. (2017, May 31). *Dowling's Clark selected to U16 National Team.* The Des Moines Register. https://www.desmoinesregister.com/story/sports/high-school/2017/05/31/dowlings-clark-selected-u-16-national-team/358824001/

Goodwin, C. (2019, February 5). *Dowling Catholic's Caitlin Clark, one of the nation's top juniors, nearly tops Iowa state record with 60 points in win.* The Des Moines Register. https://www.desmoinesregister.com/story/sports/high-school/2019/02/05/dowling-catholic-caitlin-clark-drops-60-points-win-over-mason-city-ighsau-iowa-girls-basketball/2775861002/

Graham, B. A. (2024, May 9). It won't be easy for Caitlin Clark in the WNBA, sports' most unmerciful league. *The Guardian.* https://www.theguardian.com/sport/article/2024/may/09/wnba-most-competitive-sports-league-caitlin-clark

Gregory, S. (2024, June 10). *Let Caitlin Clark live.* TIME. https://time.com/6987117/caitlin-clark-olympic-roster-wnba/

Grover, A. (2024, June 10). *Did the "Caitlin Clark effect" result in WNBA rookie's Team USA snub?* Hindustan Times. https://www.hindustantimes.com/world-news/us-news/did-caitlin-clark-effect-result-in-wnba-rookies-team-usa-snub-head-coachs-remarks-surface-amid-controversy-101717939879639.html

Gupta, D. (2023, October 20). *Iowa star Caitlin Clark recalls why playing with boys since childhood set attitude benchmark as an athlete.* Essentially Sports. https://www.essentiallysports.com/ncaa-college-basketball-news-iowa-star-caitlin-clark-recalls-why-playing-with-boys-since-childhood-set-attitude-benchmark-as-an-athlete/?token=970ec4b7067e4d95a89fac2854daf3d4

Haden, J. (2024, May 2). *Caitlin Clarks childhood shows delayed specialization is the best way to raise successful kids.* Inc. https://www.inc.com/jeff-haden/caitlin-clarks-childhood-shows-delayed-specialization-is-best-way-to-raise-successful-kids-backed-by-new-research.html?token=970ec4b7067e4d95a89fac2854daf3d4

Hall, M. L. (2023, December 7). *The Iowa State student section trolled Caitlin Clark and it (predictably) backfired.* For the Win- USA Today. https://ftw.usatoday.com/2023/12/caitlin-clark-iowa-state-3000-points-overrated-quote

Harty, P. (2023a, March 27). *A look back at when five-year old Caitlin Clark stood up to, and stood over a bully.* Hawk

Fanatic. https://hawkfanatic.com/2023/03/27/a-look-back-at-when-five-year-old-caitlin-clark-stood-up-to-and-stood-over-a-bully/?token=970ec4b7067e4d95a89fac2854daf3d4

Harty, P. (2023b, March 31). *Caitlin Clark's high school coach talks about her rise to legendary status.* Hawk Fanatic. https://hawkfanatic.com/2023/03/31/caitlin-clarks-high-school-coach-talks-about-her-rise-to-legendary-status/

Hensley, A. (2020, April 22). *Driven with confidence: How Caitlin Clark became a Hawkeye.* Sports Illustrated. https://www.si.com/college/iowa/basketball/caitlin-clark-042120

Hotchkiss, W. (2024, April 17). *Dreams coming true for Caitlin Clark and the Indiana Fever.* Fever Basketball. https://fever.wnba.com/news/dreams-coming-true-for-caitlin-clark-and-the-indiana-fever/

How tall is Caitlin Clark? Height, biography, weight, career, net worth. (2024, June 6). News Pioneer. https://newspioneer.co.uk/how-tall-is-caitlin-clark/

How to play The Chameleon. (2019, February 6). Big Potato Games. https://bigpotato.com/blogs/blog/how-to-play-the-chameleon-instructions

Hunsinger Benbow, D. (2024, April 15). *Caitlin Clark wrote future dreams down in 3rd grade. She's about to achieve one of them.* The Indianapolis Star. https://www.indystar.com/story/sports/basketball/wnba/fever/2024/04/15/caitlin-clark-wrote-her-future-dreams-down-in-3rd-grade-be-in-wnba/73100680007/

IndyStar. (2024). *Caitlin Clark's elementary school teachers watched her grow up.' She wanted to be the best, always.'.* In *YouTube.* https://youtu.be/yH1VTblf0JQ?si=LDHIZhzHRz0QUZl0

Jane, E. (2024, May 2). *Caitlin Clark raises over $100,000 for Coralville food pantry over two years.* The Daily Iowan. https://dailyiowan.com/2024/05/02/caitlin-clark-raises-over-100000-for-coralville-food-pantry-over-two-years/

Johnson, M. (2023, November 29). *How Caitlin Clark's start in West Des Moines built a homegrown star at Iowa* Pavement Pieces. https://pavementpieces.com/how-caitlin-clarks-start-in-west-des-moines-built-a-homegrown-star-at-iowa/

JWS Staff. (2023, October 15). *Caitlin Clark and Iowa set women's basketball attendance record.* Just Women's Sports. https://justwomenssports.com/reads/caitlin-clark-iowa-womens-basketball-attendance-record-outdoor-game-2023/

Karpovich, T. (2024, May 15). *Caitlin Clark finds life in WNBA not so easy.* The Epoch Times. https://www.theepochtimes.com/sports/caitlin-clark-finds-life-in-wnba-not-so-easy-5650571?utm_source=google_news_ar&utm_medium=GoogleAds&utm_campaign=reg_news_ar_0404_24_SupremeCourt&utm_term=reg_email&wall=7&gclid=CjoKCQjwsuSzBhCLARIsAIcdLm4i6SXsLB_PnYVPYrrwv_6033lNnhiCj61EAbaZZca_8Kx33q_ZBswaArJ4EALw_wcB

Kasabian, P. (2023, April 2). *Caitlin Clark: I want my legacy to be the impact I have on kids, people in Iowa.* Bleacher Report. https://bleacherreport.com/articles/10070990-caitlin-clark-i-want-my-legacy-to-be-the-impact-i-have-on-kids-people-in-iowa

Kratz, J. (2024, April 16). *Leveraging the Caitlin Clark effect for women and allies.* Forbes. https://www.forbes.com/sites/juliekratz/2024/04/16/leveraging-the-caitlin-clark-effect-for-women-and-allies/

Lawhon, D. (2019, February 25). *Class 5A hoops: Dowling outlasts Waukee in 3OT classic as Clark sets class tournament record.* The Des Moines Register. https://www.desmoinesregister.com/story/sports/high-school/2019/02/25/iowa-basketball-high-school-girls-state-tournament-2019-waukee-caitlin-clark-dowling-catholic/2976237002/

Legend of Caitlin Clark began with competitive, sometimes bloody Nerf basketball battles against her brothers. (2024, February 15). KCCI Des Moines. https://www.kcci.com/article/iowa-basketball-caitlin-clark-ncaa-scoring-record/46662031?utm_source=ground.news&utm_medium=referral

Leistikow, C. (2021, August 20). *With an eye on the Final Four, Caitlin Clark's Iowa story is just beginning.* Hawk Central. https://www.hawkcentral.com/story/sports/college/columnists/chad-leistikow/2021/08/20/caitlin-clark-basketball-iowa-olympics-gold-medal-nil-shirt-final-four/8187769002/

Lemoncelli, J. (2024, July 1). *Diana Taurasi praises Caitlin Clark after first battle in Fever win.* NY Post. https://nypost.com/2024/07/01/sports/diana-taurasi-praises-caitlin-clark-after-first-battle-in-fever-win/

Li, D. K. (2024, June 11). *WNBA attendance is skyrocketing—and it's not all on Caitlin Clark.* NBC News. https://www.nbcnews.com/news/sports/wnba-attendance-skyrocketing-not-caitlin-clark-rcna156422

Linder, J. (2020, April 24). *Caitlin Clark ready to take the keys at point guard for Iowa women's basketball.* The Gazette. https://www.thegazette.com/sports/caitlin-clark-ready-to-take-the-keys-at-point-guard-for-iowa-womens-basketball/

Logan, E. (2024, April 23). *Caitlin Clark just landed a $28 million deal with Nike—and her own shoe.* Glamour. https://www.glamour.com/story/caitlin-clark-just-landed-a-dollar28-million-deal-with-nike-and-her-own-shoe

Maciaszek, M. (2024, May 21). *Basketball Star Caitlin Clark partners with Wilson.* National Sporting Goods Association. https://nsga.org/news/basketball-star-caitlin-clark-partners-with-wilson/

Mack, J. L. (2024, June 13). *Caitlin Clark's wild first month in the WNBA.* Axios Indianapolis. https://www.axios.com/local/indianapolis/2024/06/13/caitlin-clark-first-month-wnba-fever

Maloney, J. (2024, April 17). *Caitlin Clark officially declares for 2024 WNBA Draft: Iowa star expected to go No. 1 to Fever.* CBS Sports. https://www.cbssports.com/wnba/news/caitlin-clark-officially-declares-for-2024-wnba-draft-iowa-star-expected-to-go-no-1-to-fever/#:~:text=Iowa%20star%20Caitlin%20Clark%20announced

Mann, B. (2024, June 9). *WNBA star Caitlin Clark doesn't make the USA Olympics basketball team.* NPR. https://www.npr.org/2024/06/09/nx-s1-4997705/caitlin-clark-olympics-basketball-wnba

Marsh, C. (2024, May 2). *4 things we want to see from Caitlin Clark's first Nike signature sneakers.* GQ. https://www.gq.com/story/caitlin-clark-nike-deal-first-signature-sneaker

Marshall, J. (2024, March 26). *Be like Caitlin: Iowa's Caitlin Clark is inspiring a younger generation of players.* AP News. https://apnews.com/article/caitlin-clark-march-madness-66d3a911f32cb9081acf1a21b9a79d6f

McCarthy, C. (2024, May 14). *Caitlin Clark wears $1,500 Tiffany & Co x Nike sneakers to WNBA debut.* NY Post. https://nypost.com/2024/05/14/sports/caitlin-clark-wears-1500-tiffany-amp-co-x-nike-sneakers-to-wnba-debut/

McCaskill, S. (2024, April 9). *NCAA women's march madness final secures record 18.7m viewers.* SportsPro. https://www.sportspromedia.com/news/march-madness-south-carolina-iowa-basketball-caitlin-clark/

McGregor, G. (2024, May 25). *What sneaker is Caitlin Clark wearing? Tracking Nike shoes worn by Fever star rookie.* Sporting News. https://www.sportingnews.com/us/wnba/news/what-nike-sneaker-caitlin-clark-tracking-fever-rookie/32539a953d9526c1bbd61758

McKessy, J. (2024, June 20). *Caitlin Clark told Indiana fever head coach that team USA snub "woke a monster."* USA TODAY. https://www.usatoday.com/story/sports/wnba/fever/2024/06/09/caitlin-clark-fever-olympics-snub-woke-monster/74037580007/

Menezes, D. (2024, April 6). *Caitlin Clark's high school coach calls superstar "a goofball off-court."* News Nation. https://www.newsnationnow.com/us-news/sports/caitlin-clark-coach-goofball-off-court/

Mina, A. C. (2024, May 15). *Caitlin Clark makes a glamorous WNBA debut sporting luxury sneakers.* Under the Laces. https://underthelaces.com/posts/caitlin-clark-wears-tiffany-and-co-nike-air-force-ones-wnba-debut-01hxzeynfb08

Morey, J. (2024, April 15). *10 things to know about Caitlin Clark.* WNBA Fever. https://fever.wnba.com/news/10-things-to-know-about-caitlin-clark/

Murphy Jr., B. (2024, June 24). *With 5 short words, Caitlin Clark just taught a powerful lesson in emotional intelligence.* Inc. https://www.inc.com/bill-murphy-jr/caitlin-clark-wnba-indiana-fever-everybody-just-loves-instant-satisfaction.html

Murrey, B. (2024, March 21). *Clarkonomics: The impact of Caitlin Clark & Hawkeye women's basketball on Iowa's economy.* Common Sense Institute Iowa. https://commonsenseinstituteia.org/clarkonomics/

Nagel, C. (2024, May 25). *Caitlin Clark avoiding social media drama, focusing on mental health in transition to WNBA.* 247Sports. https://247sports.com/article/caitlin-clark-avoiding-social-media-drama-focusing-on-mental-health-in-transition-to-wnba-232167185/

Naughton, J. (2018a, February 21). *Iowa high school star Caitlin Clark seeks a normal kid life while being sought by college elite.* USA Today. https://usatodayhss.com/2018/iowa-high-school-star-caitlin-clark-seeks-a-normal-kid-life-while-being-sought-by-college-elite

Naughton, J. (2018b, March 1). *Meet the register's 2017-18 All-CIML girls' basketball team.* The Des Moines Register. https://www.desmoinesregister.com/story/sports/high-school/2018/03/01/meet-registers-2017-2018-all-ciml-girls-basketball-team/384422002/

Nordstrom, L. (2024, April 20). *Caitlin Clark's stylist on why her viral WNBA draft Prada look is just the beginning.* Women's Wear Daily. https://wwd.com/eye/people/caitlin-clark-stylist-prada-louis-vuitton-fashion-style-1236322846/?utm_source=Twitter&utm_campaign=Twitter-WWD&utm_medium=social

O'Hara, S. (2024, May 8). *"She's really inspiring": Caitlin Clark's impact on the next generation of basketball players.* Fox 59. https://fox59.com/news/shes-really-inspiring-caitlin-clarks-impact-on-the-next-generation-of-basketball-players/

Olson, E. (2024, February 6). *Caitlin Clark was a grade-school phenom. Her 60-point game in high school was sign of things to come.* AP News. https://apnews.com/article/caitlin-clark-iowa-9832f708e5a2590b7865c0ffd9f2375e

Opiyo, C. (2024a, January 20). *Why did Caitlin Clark go to Iowa? Exploring the star guard's reasons for choosing the Hawkeyes.* Sportskeeda. https://www.sportskeeda.com/college-basketball/why-caitlin-clark-go-iowa-exploring-star-guard-s-reasons-choosing-hawkeyes

Opiyo, C. (2024b, March 15). *Gatorade donates $25,000 to Caitlin Clark's foundation after Iowa's big win against Nebraska.* Sportskeeda. https://www.sportskeeda.com/college-basketball/news-reports-gatorade-donates-25-000-caitlin-clark-s-foundation-iowa-s-big-win-nebraska

Perreault, D. (2024, February 16). *How Caitlin Clark is inspiring the next generation of female athletes.* KWWL. https://www.kwwl.com/sports/iowa-hawkeyes/how-caitlin-clark-is-inspiring-the-next-generation-of-female-athletes/article_2b8a1738-cd29-11ee-b7ba-57f01eece3ba.html

Phelps, C. (2024, June 21). *Caitlin Clark makes WNBA history against Atlanta Dream.* Athlon Sports. https://athlonsports.com/wnba/caitlin-clark-makes-wnba-history-against-atlanta-dream

Philippou, A. (2024, April 15). *Clark goes first to fever, leads "generational class."* ESPN. https://www.espn.com/wnba/story/_/id/39951045/indiana-fever-select-iowa-caitlin-clark-top-pick-2024-wnba-draft

Piccotti, T. (2024, April 4). *Get to know Caitlin Clark, the record-setting NCAA hoops superstar as she heads to the*

REFERENCES

WNBA. Biography. https://www.biography.com/athletes/a43455833/caitlin-clark-march-madness?token=970ec4b7067e4d95a89fac2854daf3d4

Pickman, B. (2024a, May 20). *What we learned from Caitlin Clark's first week in the WNBA*. The Athletic. https://www.nytimes.com/athletic/5505122/2024/05/20/caitlin-clark-first-week-wnba-fever/?ds_c=7170000119025978&site=google&network=g&campaign_

Pickman, B. (2024b, June 3). *Caitlin Clark wins WNBA Rookie of the month for first 9 games with Fever*. The Athletic. https://www.nytimes.com/athletic/5538206/2024/06/03/cailtin-clark-wnba-rookie-of-month/

Polacek, S. (n.d.). *Tracking Caitlin Clark's stats, top highlights for 2024 WNBA rookie season with Fever*. Bleacher Report. https://bleacherreport.com/articles/10121114-tracking-caitlin-clarks-stats-top-highlights-for-2024-wnba-rookie-season-with-fever

Postrado, J. (2024, May 12). *How Fever's Caitlin Clark became a "powerful" role model amid Iowa spotlight*. ClutchPoints. https://clutchpoints.com/fever-news-how-caitlin-clark-became-a-powerful-role-model-amid-iowa-spotlight

Reedy, J. (2024, April 2). *Iowa's victory over LSU is the most-watched women's college basketball game on record*. AP News. https://apnews.com/article/march-madness-iowa-caitlin-clark-ratings-c60cf8dc950f8b33fd37aab7ca3fc487

Saunders, A. (2024, April 18). *Caitlin Clark's high school coach says "I don't think anyone could have predicted" her success*. People. https://people.com/caitlin-clarks-high-school-coach-reflects-on-her-success-8635251

Schnell, L. (2024, June 13). *Caitlin Clark is tired, and for good reason. Breaking down WNBA's tough opening schedule*. USA Today. https://www.usatoday.com/story/sports/wnba/2024/06/13/wnba-schedule-caitlin-clark-tired/73986302007/

Schutte, D. (2024, April 17). *Caitlin Clark trusts Indiana Fever teammates*. Women's Fastbreak on SI. https://www.si.com/onsi/womens-fastbreak/analysis/posts/caitlin-clark-trusts-indiana-fever-teammates-01j13jsgtft1

Sullivan, B. (2024, April 2). *Caitlin Clark once dreamed of going to UConn. Now, she'll face them in the final four*. NPR. https://www.npr.org/2024/04/02/1242334968/caitlin-clark-iowa-uconn-final-four

Sykes II, M. D. (2024, April 2). *Caitlin Clark's incredibly accurate pass to her brother after beating LSU may have been her best assist*. USA Today. https://ftw.usatoday.com/lists/caitlin-clarks-incredibly-accurate-pass-to-her-brother-after-beating-lsu-may-have-been-her-best-assist

t2023/24 Initiatives. (n.d.). The Caitlin Clark Foundation. https://caitlinclarkfoundation.org/

Tam, N. (2023, April 5). *Caitlin Clark inspires young Iowans to play basketball*. KCCI. https://www.kcci.com/article/caitlin-clark-inspires-young-iowans-basketball/43524547

Tempera, J. (2024, April 8). *Here's how Caitlin Clark paid tribute to the Hawkeyes after heartbreaking loss*. Women's Health. https://www.womenshealthmag.com/life/a46802918/caitlin-clark-wnba/

Thirty eight Caitlin Clark quotes about women's basketball, Iowa, & success. (2024). Basketball Mindset Training. https://www.basketballmindsettraining.com/blog/caitlin-clark-quotes

Thomas, M. (2023, May 23). *Caitlin Clark: Biography, career, top stories for the women's college basketball star*. Sportscasting Athlete Index. https://www.sportscasting.com/caitlin-clark-biography-career-top-stories-for-the-womens-college-basketball-star/?token=970ec4b7067e4d95a89fac2854daf3d4

Thompson, W. (2024, March 20). *Being Caitlin Clark: Inside the world of the player who redefined the game*. ESPN. https://www.espn.com/womens-college-basketball/story/_/id/39740282/caitlin-clark-iowa-2024-ncaa-women-basketball-tournament-ready-march

Torok, N. (2024, May 3). *How Caitlin Clark is changing the world, both on and off the court.* The Science Survey. https://thesciencesurvey.com/sports/2024/05/13/how-caitlin-clark-is-changing-the-world-both-on-and-off-court/

Turbett, J. (2024, June 5). *Must-have gear from Caitlin Clark's NIL deals.* Clutch Buys. https://buy.clutchpoints.com/must-have-gear-from-caitlin-clarks-nil-deals

Valora, C., & Thomas, S. (2024, March 29). *Inside the shoe game of Iowa basketball star Caitlin Clark.* Iowa Magazine. https://magazine.foriowa.org/story.php?ed=true&storyid=2419

Verry, P. (2024, May 14). *What Nike sneaker will Caitlin Clark wear in her WNBA debut?* Yahoo Sports. https://sports.yahoo.com/sneaker-caitlin-clark-wear-her-210744069.html

Villa, W. (2017, May 30). *After a measured approach to trials, recruit Caitlin Clark riding high with USA basketball.* ESPN. https://www.espn.com/espnw/sports/story/_/id/19577932/dowling-catholic-caitlin-clark-rides-athleticism-usa-basketball-roster-spot-fiba-americas-argentina

Voepel, M. (2022, November 18). *Iowa star Clark day-to-day after injuring ankle.* ESPN.com. https://www.espn.com/womens-college-basketball/story/_/id/35051395/iowa-caitlin-clark-injured-upset-loss-kansas-state

Walsh, K. (2024, May 22). *Caitlin Clark just signed the Michael Jordan of endorsement deals. Literally.* Glamour. https://www.glamour.com/story/caitlin-clark-just-signed-michael-jordan-endorsement-deals-literally

Williams, B. (2024, May 11). *Inside Caitlin Clark's incredible lifestyle as she becomes face of WNBA.* The US Sun. https://www.the-sun.com/sport/11313651/inside-caitlin-clark-incredible-lifestyle-wnba-indiana-fever/

Williams, M. (2024, June 24). *L.A. Olympics exec. Thinks Team USA missed an opportunity to select Caitlin Clark.* SI. https://www.si.com/wnba/la-olympics-exec-thinks-team-usa-missed-an-opportunity-to-select-caitlin-clark

Wolken, D. (2024, June 22). *Forget the online rancor, Caitlin Clark helping WNBA break through to fans of all ages.* USA TODAY. https://www.usatoday.com/story/sports/columnist/dan-wolken/2024/06/21/wnba-caitlin-clark-excitement-sold-out-crowd-atlanta/74177441007/

Young, G. (2024, May 16). *Brothers "were just awful" to Caitlin Clark growing up.* Heavy. https://heavy.com/sports/wnba/caitlin-clark-mom-brothers-awful-childhood/

Youth sports facts: Why youth sports matter. (n.d.). Project Play. https://projectplay.org/youth-sports/facts?token=970ec4b7067e4d95a89fac2854daf3d4

Zucker, J. (2024a, May 23). *Photos of Caitlin Clark's Kobe Bryant shoes worn in WNBA games to open Fever career.* Bleacher Report. https://bleacherreport.com/articles/10122310-photos-of-caitlin-clarks-kobe-bryant-shoes-worn-in-wnba-games-to-open-fever-career

Zucker, J. (2024b, June 16). *Caitlin Clark talks mental health before game vs. Angel Reese, Carter, Sky.* Bleacher Report. https://bleacherreport.com/articles/10125019-video-caitlin-clark-talks-mental-health-before-game-vs-angel-reese-carter-sky#:~:text=Clark%20emphasized%20the%20broad%20importance

Made in United States
Orlando, FL
19 December 2024

56218729R10050